PSYCHIC READING

PSYCHIC READING

Two Dramatic Dialogues

BY T.C. EISELE

REBEL SATORI PRESS
New Orleans

Lao Tzu quote from the *Tao Te Ching* on page 41 translated by J.H. McDonald for the public domain

Book Design: Sven Davisson
Cover Illustration: Corinne Alexis Hall

ISBN: 978-1-60864-125-3

Rebel Satori Press
www.rebelsatoripress.com

To all the people over the last 17 years
Who have come to me for help-
You have given my life its purpose,
Thank you

And once again,

For Diana

♥

"Even though they are equally human, there are so-called great people who match their qualities with heaven and earth. Try examining your own mind and your own nature – how may they match heaven and earth? If they match, then be diligent; if not, then quickly reform. Do this, and attaining human greatness will not be a worry."

—Anthology on the Cultivation of Realization,
Ming Dynasty 1739, Author Unknown

"'I' is the most hazardous place in the world."
—J.G. Bennett

"Learning how to operate a soul figures to take time."
—Timothy Leary

CONTENTS

INTRODUCTION

The book you are about to read presents the dialogue for a pair of Psychic Readings. While both of these encounters are fictional creations, the material in them is based upon thousands of actual client sessions that I conducted as a Professional Psychic, Astrologer, and Tarot Reader in New York City over a period of more than 17 years.

What is a Psychic Reading? The act of going to a special individual for spiritual and/or esoteric guidance has existed in one form or another since ancient times and, depending on the cultural setting, could have included activities as varied as making a pilgrimage to the oracle at Delphi in Ancient Greece, consulting a tribal Shaman, or visiting the local Witch on the outskirts of town. Yet regardless of the setting, exactly who are these special people we ask to impart to us their visions and wisdom? In what ways are they different from the rest of us? How do they manage to acquire the insights they are sharing? What does it mean to be Psychic?

The human brain is perhaps the most profound Machine in the Universe, but where do our thoughts come from? We each possess consciousness, but what is our awareness made of? Modern Physiology will tell us that we use only 10% of our brain's capacity, which would then mean that 90% of our mind's potential remains dormant within us. If that is the case, then perhaps in the same way that the genetics for an entire tree can exist within a tiny acorn, maybe all the secrets of the universe can also be explained within the untapped portions of the human mind? If this is true, then maybe the Gurus and Psychics we go to for insights are really nothing more than normal people like ourselves who have found a way to activate more than 10% of their innate intelligence? Maybe the late Psychologist and Philosopher Timothy Leary was right when he said, "The Brain is God"?

Clairvoyance, clairaudience, and clairsentience, or the abilities to see, hear, or perceive expanded realities and non-ordinary states of being are among the sorts of powers commonly considered Psychic, yet the relative truth of these experiences are extremely difficult to verify, or even comprehend in terms of conventional understanding. To the general public the popular idea of a Psychic is someone dressed up like a gypsy or a witch who predicts the future using Tarot Cards and a crystal ball. However, if one can manage to put such stereotypes aside the actual truth is that real Psychics, while in possession of one or more of the aforementioned abilities, are also often highly trained individuals in an Esoteric/Occult sense who are capable of offering valuable insights and guidance to those who are in psychological or spiritual crisis.

Because of its counseling-like format, a legitimate Psychic Reading can sometimes be looked upon as a form of Psychotherapy, yet the distinction should be made that a Reading is not Psychotherapy. Where Therapy encourages a Client to take the lead and share their fears and neuroses with the Practitioner over an extended period of time, a Psychic Reading operates under a very definite time constraint and on a much different level. While a Psychotherapist will mostly listen and occasionally direct the Client with a comment or leading question, the whole purpose of a Psychic Reading is for the Reader to cut directly to the chase and provide the client with immediate insights to digest . This is possible because of the Reader's unique abilities that allow him or her to quickly perceive the Client's issues. As a result, in my work as a Psychic Counselor I do not consider the service I offer to be a long term one. If I have done my job properly then a client does not need to see me more than once or twice a year except under certain circumstances. Once a Reading is over though it is essential for the Client to continue exploring what was revealed in the session in order to be able to transform their daily behavior and eliminate non-productive patterns from their lives. It is in providing this sort of follow-up process over a longer period of time that essentially constitutes the role of Psychotherapy. The essential difference then between a Psychic Reading and Psychotherapy would be that a Reading opens a door for the client, while Therapy is designed to help the individual adjust over time to the new room they have chosen to enter.

Another important matter regarding Psychic Readings that should be discussed is the difference between Psychic abilities and Spiritual evolution. I have been talking about what it means to be Psychic, but what does it mean to be Spiritual? Over the course of my career as a Reader I have come to believe that to be Spiritual simply means to recognize that the evolving interests of both the individual and the collective have a unified purpose. Such an understanding can be developed in any number of ways, thus the famous saying, "Paths are many, but the truth is one." Nevertheless, the common misunderstanding shared by many people is that Psychic abilities are the basis for Spiritual understanding, when in fact it is usually the opposite. Once a Spiritual perspective has been developed according to the inner work that is required in most esoteric traditions, it is likely that Psychic Powers will naturally develop as a matter of course. On the other hand, there are those individuals who have been blessed with natural Psychic abilities who end up becoming nothing more than performers or hustlers looking only to profit from their talents without ever considering any sort of ethical or spiritual foundation. The danger with such an opportunistic approach is that until the ego is properly managed and one's Psychic gifts are practiced with both humility and a concern for the general welfare, Psychic power explored for its own sake will only be a fuel for arrogance and the common pitfalls of vanity. With this in mind, it is therefore extremely important for a quality Psychic Reading to always include a substantial amount of ethical teaching, compassionate understanding, and good common sense as a reflection of the Reader's Spiritual Maturity.

The next matter I would like to address is controversial in that it concerns the negative or superstitious aspects sometimes associated with Psychic Readings, namely the power and influence of evil forces as well as the overwhelming tendency for people to believe what they want to, regardless of what may or may not actually be happening.

Over the years individuals have approached me from time to time to share that another Psychic has told them they are cursed. I usually explain to these people that anyone who would tell them that is a Con Artist not a Psychic and the whole thing is nothing more than a scam designed to hustle a fee for getting rid of the curse. While this might sound simple enough to anyone reading this, how is it possible for such a situation to occur? Why would otherwise intelligent people believe such nonsense? Unfortunately, many people who are going for readings are doing so for the wrong reasons. Going to a Psychic to deal with fears about the future or hoping that one's problems can be made to magickally disappear is asking for trouble, for it is that kind of desperation that allows any Charlatan who is posing as a Psychic to exploit the situation by suggesting that dark and malevolent forces rather than personal responsibility are at the root of what is occurring. Needless to say, Readers who prey on people in this fashion are criminals and need to be dealt with accordingly. The problem though is that by the time a Client comes to me about something like this they are either totally freaked out or else too embarrassed to want to do anything about it. As a result our subsequent session usually ends up focusing on how they can forgive themselves for being so naïve.

Another type of unfortunate situation that can exist in a Reading is when a Psychic is willing to tell a Client whatever they want to hear in order to take their money. The most common example of this is when someone can't let go of a romantic partner and the Reader will have them returning for session after session, assuring them that the individual they are asking about is really their soul mate and the relationship is destined to have a happy ending. Of course this is the worst sort of manipulation and often ends with either the client eventually catching on (if they don't run out of money first) or with the Reader ironically becoming annoyed by the neurotic behavior they have agreed to indulge.

Though it has pained me to mention these negative aspects of my Profession, I have done so only because I believe it needs to be made known that going for a Psychic Reading is very much a situation of "let the buyer beware." On the other hand, I also believe there are many honorable practitioners out there and it is entirely possible to receive an enlightening reading from a legitimate Psychic if one is willing to do their research and ask around. As a Reader I have never advertised and usually only accept clients by referral. I have chosen to run my practice in this way because I believe it creates a safe guard for myself as well as for those I work with. This does not mean that a Reader who advertises can't be trusted. It just needs to be kept in mind that much of advertising in general can be dishonest and it is no different with Psychics.

In closing I would like to say that every effort has been made in this current work to reproduce the experience of a Psychic Reading as authentically as possible. I only hope that I have managed to do justice to the very real therapeutic value of an ancient form of healing that is, unfortunately, still largely misrepresented and misunderstood

Woodhaven, NY 2017

FIRST READING

CHARACTERS

The Reader

A slim, slightly graying man in his fifties
dressed casually in black

The Client (Mary)

An attractive, stylish, professional woman
in her late twenties

Scene:

In the center of a dimly lit, cozy room a table and two chairs are situated in front of an overflowing bookcase. One of the chairs is a comfortable looking, black lounger and the other is a simple, straight-back dining room chair. A black cloth with a pattern of gold pentagrams covers the table, upon which a white votive candle is burning next to a black velvet bag and a pair of old, heavy looking books stacked one on top of the other. An antique reading lamp is also on the table and a collection of esoteric pictures and sacred symbols adorn the walls. There is a thick burgundy curtain covering the entranceway and in the far corner of the room on another, smaller table is an incense burner that emits a thin plume of smoke that makes the entire space smell like a church.

After a few moments The Reader enters through the curtain and then holds it open for The Client as she comes in behind him. The Reader then directs The Client to sit in the dining room chair and after they are both seated he begins speaking.

READER: Thanks for coming Mary…. What would you like to know?

MARY: I've never done this before, so I don't know what's supposed to happen. Do I ask you a question and then you tell me the future?

READER: If I could predict the future do you think I'd be in this place and charging these prices? (Mary smiles) No one can predict the future. When people come to see me it's usually because something in their life isn't working. That's not a matter of the future it's a matter of the present. So what would you like to see working better in your life?

MARY: My love life, I guess?

READER: Are you in a relationship?

MARY: Sort of...

READER: "Sort of " is always interesting...how long have you been in this situation?

MARY: Pretty close to a year.

READER: What do you do?

MARY: You mean for a living?

READER: Yes.

MARY: I work in Fashion Design.

READER: Do you like it?

MARY: I love it!

READER: Okay, then let's talk about your love life.

(The Reader reaches over and picks up one of the two large books situated on the table and proceeds to open it.)

Let's begin by looking at your birthday. What is it?

MARY: March 4, 1987

(The Reader flips through the pages of the book until he comes to the one he is looking for)

READER: Do you know if you were born before or after 12 noon?

MARY: Not really, but I think it was in the morning.

READER: That's okay, don't guess, according to the Ephemeris you have a Taurus Moon no matter how we slice the pie.

MARY: Is that good?

READER: It's neither good nor bad, it just indicates where the Moon was on the day you were born. The Moon symbolizes your emotions and the sign it's in represents your particular emotional style, which in this case is Taurus, the sign of comfort, stability, and practicality. You also have a Pisces Sun in relatively good aspect to your Moon. That means both planets were having a productive conversation of energies at the time of your birth.

MARY: I'm sorry, but I really don't understand what any of this means.

READER: Okay, let me start at the beginning. Each of the Planets in Astrology is supposed to represent a different archetype of human behavior. For instance, Venus is your love nature, Mars your physical nature, etc. We then look at where the planets were at the moment you were born and based on their relationships to one another a general map of your personality can be constructed.

Of course after the moment of your birth the planets

continued moving, so the practice of Astrology, what we're doing here, consists of comparing the current or "transiting" positions of the planets to the original positions at the time of your birth in order to see what cycles of activity are coming into play.

MARY: I understand, but it still sounds complicated.

READER: No worries, I'll interpret for you what's going on…Your Pisces Sun would indicate an empathetic nature and an artistic temperament, while the Taurus Moon would speak to a need for emotional security; as a result, I would venture to say you endeavor to be a good partner and would prefer to be in a stable, long term relationship as opposed to just casually dating. Your Moon is also conjunct with Mars, or action, and opposes Pluto in Scorpio, or desire and transformation, with both ends of the opposition in turn squaring Venus in Aquarius, or universal love. A line-up like that could cause you to struggle relentlessly for approval in your relationships. You have Neptune, or illusion, involved in all this as well in the sign of Capricorn, which makes you think you have to be the one who is responsible for everyone else in your life. In other words, you feel guilty about not doing enough so you put up with far more than you should.

MARY: Wow… that's sounds exactly right.

READER: You also have Jupiter sextile Venus, which means you're lucky, although I think your luck works better for others than it does for you.

MARY: That's funny.

READER: Why?

MARY: Because I've never felt lucky, but it's an interesting way of putting it. I guess that might explain why I usually feel like I never get back as much as I give.

READER: Good deduction! You have Saturn in Sagittarius as well, meaning you'll be getting your first Saturn return later this year, which would probably make this the perfect time to ask yourself why you feel that way.

MARY: What's a Saturn return?

READER: It takes Saturn approximately 28 years to go around the entire zodiac and return to the exact place it was when you were born. During the course of your life you'll likely get to experience 3 of these returns. The first one happens at around age 28 and represents the first realization of responsibility, or accepting that the circumstances of your life are up to you. The second return happens at about age 56 and coincides with the male and female menopause. The last one occurs near age 84 and that's usually about starting to consider what may come after this life, that is, if you're still around.

MARY: Wow, that all sounds pretty significant, which makes sense because I'm feeling a lot more urgency about where I'm going in my life than I have in the past.

READER: Saturn has just recently entered the sign of Sagittarius; so right now it's squaring your Mercury in early Pisces and challenging a tendency you have to think more with your emotions than your intellect. This will probably create a great deal of frustration, as you will be forced to be more objective than usual. Mercury is also about communication, so if you're not currently expressing your needs in a proper way then misunderstandings in your relationships could be the result of this current push from Saturn.

MARY: That also sounds like what I'm going through. Nothing quite feels right in my personal life and I don't know what to do about it.

READER: Before this current guy you're "sort of" involved with, when was your last serious relationship? How long ago?

MARY: I was in a long-term relationship for about 3 years and it ended about 3 months before I met the guy I'm currently seeing.

READER: What's the first initial of the guy you were with for 3 years?

MARY: What do you mean?

READER: The first letter of his first name.

MARY: Oh, T.

(Closing his eyes, the Reader sits back in his chair, takes a deep breath, and sits perfectly still. After a moment he begins to move his hands rhythmically, making it appear as if he is sewing with an invisible needle and thread. He continues with these movements for several seconds before stopping and speaking.)

READER: You were with this guy for 3 years, how long did it take before you realized how self-absorbed he is?

MARY: Pretty soon after we were together.

READER: (The Reader looks at her questioningly and then resumes speaking) He also didn't express his emotions very well, did he?

MARY: Nope

READER: So the majority of your time with him was spent filling in the blanks to try and figure out what he wasn't communicating?

MARY: That's right.........what a waste of time, huh?

READER: He only ever opened up when he needed something...then you were relieved and thought that at least for a bit he seemed accessible and maybe things would change?

MARY: Oh my God, were you there? (She then laughs, but not because she thought her comment was funny).

READER: So in essence the relationship only continued because you worked at it?

MARY: I'm afraid so.

READER: Let me ask you a question. Do you think you are worthy of love without having to do anything for it?

MARY: Could you say that again?

READER: Do you think you are worthy of love without having to do anything for it?

MARY: I'm not sure I understand.... Don't they say you're supposed to work at having a good relationship?

READER: Let's put it this way, anyone that could truly love you doesn't need you to do anything other than to be yourself, correct?

MARY: That's true.

READER: (He stares at Mary for a couple of seconds.)

You were frustrated during a good deal of that relationship, but instead of admitting your anger to yourself and leaving, you thought trying to fix him would make you feel better… well, did it?

MARY: At first, but then after a while it made me feel stupid.

READER: But we both know you're not stupid…. The really frustrating part in all this was his passive aggressive attitude, like he was listening to you, when in fact he would just not respond and then continue doing the same crap over and over like a spoiled kid. When did it occur to you that this dynamic was transforming you from his girlfriend into his mother?

MARY: OH MY GOD!!! You are so right! It drove me nuts!

READER: Yeah, we are currently in the throes of a world wide epidemic of what I refer to as "man-boys". The young men in this current generation have been spoiled rotten. They are self-entitled, emotionally irresponsible, and in the end it's always about them. I never cease to be amazed at how many otherwise intelligent women fall for this and get suckered into being their surrogate mothers. Nevertheless, in a grander sense everything is exactly the way it should be.

MARY: I don't understand?

READER: My humble theory on why people come together is because each of us holds the key to another person's lessons, and that's irresistible. There is no accounting for taste, so we all go for the prettiest package we can find. The simple fact though is that we are ultimately attracted to someone who is going to help us evolve. An accommodating person like yourself who can be made to feel guilty will usually end up with someone self-absorbed who will take advantage of you. The idea behind this is that you will eventually stand up for yourself and the other person will learn to be more considerate. Usually though no one learns anything without years of making the same mistakes over and over. This state of affairs brings me a lot of business, but I'm not gloating about it. You know the French Poet Rimbaud once said, "A battle of the soul is as brutal as a battle of men" and he was right, which is why most people would prefer to ride a seesaw of familiar circumstances back and forth between titillation and pain rather than take a hard look at themselves in the mirror.

MARY: So how can I change? What do I do?

READER: By asking that question you have already started the process, so let's go deeper. How do you get along with your parents?

MARY: Fine, I guess.

READER: Really?

MARY: Okay, sometimes it's hard to talk with them, especially my Mother.

READER: Are they both still alive?

MARY: Yes

READER: Are they still together?

MARY: Yes

READER: What is your Father's first initial?

MARY: T

(The Reader raises his eyebrows and Mary acknowledges his expression with a sheepish, half-smile.)

READER: And your Mother's first initial?

MARY: B

(The Reader takes a breath, centers himself, and then begins his mysterious hand movements. This goes on for a few moments, after which he stops and stares blankly to his right. A short silence follows and then he speaks.)

READER: While it may be hard to talk with your Mom, you've completely given up with your Dad except for basic politeness.

MARY: (She leans forward as though about to speak, but then gives a little wave while seeming to hold back tears.)

I'm sorry for getting emotional....

READER: That's quite all right. Don't worry about it.

(The Reader reaches over and takes a box of tissues from

the bookcase and offers it to Mary)

MARY: No thank you, I'm okay.

(After putting the tissues back, The Reader allows Mary a moment to regain her composure before he continues.)

READER: Your parents have a very traditional relationship in so far as your Dad is all about his job and your Mom takes care of everything else. What does your Father do for a living?

MARY: He's a Banker.

READER: He's also not an emotionally accessible person. This was tough for you as a little girl. Your Father provided material comfort, yet he never seemed to notice your longing for a deeper sense of safety on an emotional level. If it makes you feel any better your Mom has the same difficulty with him. She takes care of everything in order to gain his approval, but he was never very demonstrative with her either. He takes her efforts for granted and criticizes her quite often. You have sensed your Mom's unhappiness for a long time. Their dynamic is very confusing for you, yet it has become your relationship model.

MARY: Is that why I can't seem to find the right guy?

READER: Perhaps...you long to please your Father so you will seek out men like him, but it's your Mother you're really angry with. You see her as weak, but you're just like her. As a result, you've come to see your own loving and cooperative nature as weakness.

(The Reader sits in silence for a moment to let what he

has said sink in.)

What hope do any of us have at finding love if we come to view sensitivity as weakness and selfishness as strength? For too long you have seen your vulnerability as a fault when in actuality it is the seed of your strength. You need to realize that only strong people can open their hearts.

MARY: Whenever I've tried to open my heart I've been hurt. The men I've been with just take advantage of me when I'm nice, then when I need them to understand they accuse me of being selfish.

READER: You don't need any lessons on how to be selfless; you need to work on drawing some boundaries so selfish people can no longer take advantage of you.

MARY: So I should probably begin by telling this guy I'm seeing now that I deserve more of a commitment from his immature ass!

(Mary's mood suddenly turns lighter as she laughs at her own declaration)

READER: There you go, like the song say's "R-e-s-p-e-c-t".

(The Reader and Mary laugh together for a few moments, yet once their laughter has subsided, Mary continues in a more somber tone.)

MARY: I know I need to change.

READER: I agree. The question however is, how much are you willing to let a relationship change you?

MARY: A lot, it would seem. I've been willing to do almost anything that my partners have demanded rather than just saying "no" and being by myself until someone better came along.

READER: You know you really can't say you've let any of your relationships change you if you've done the same thing in every one of them. What usually happens with you is that rather than trying to change what you do, you instead try to change the relationship by attempting to fix your partner.

If you really want to let a relationship change you, then risk telling this new guy what you need. If he doesn't deliver, you walk. Not a year later, but as soon as you know it's not right…. And don't try to fix anything! Now that would be letting a relationship change you because you'd be doing something completely different than you ever have before.

(For a few moments Mary stares blankly into space before the Reader resumes speaking)

What is the first initial of this guy you are currently seeing?

MARY: What? Oh, sorry….it's T, his initial is T.

(The Reader and Mary exchange meaningful glances with one another)

READER: Wow, a trifecta!

MARY: Yes, I know, the names of all the men in my life begin with T.

(The Reader calms himself once again and then does his mysterious, rhythmic hand mudras.)

READER: What does this current "T" do?

MARY: He's a musician

READER: All I'll say here is that you're dating the same type of guy you've always dated. Perhaps he has a different haircut, maybe a mustache, he might even be skinnier than the last guy, but essentially it's the same emotionally inaccessible energy as your Father.

MARY: Wow! The guy I'm with now is skinny and has a mustache, but my ex was husky and clean-shaven. That's so funny!

READER: In some ways though this current guy is a little different. He has forced himself to be aloof, but deep down he's really more sensitive. Growing up he had to contend with a Father who is very much like yours. To survive he learned to be just like his Daddy and fight insensitivity with insensitivity. In reality he's not emotionless, he's just a chicken when it comes to letting anyone know how he feels.

MARY: I can see that about him.

READER: Let's get back to what I mentioned before about you drawing boundaries. Maybe it would be scary at first to be alone after standing up for yourself, but you wouldn't really be alone, you'd be free. The fear would only be the realization that you'd made a decision of your own free will and now you're responsible for the consequences.

MARY: It just seems scary. What if no one wants me the way I really am?

READER: Forgive me for saying this, but you don't know who you really are. You know what others expectations of you have been, but which of those roles you've played would you say is the real you? Which of those versions was a whole and confident person? And which of those roles has gotten you what you really want?

MARY: None of them, I guess? But what about something like The Secret? Should I be reminding myself everyday what I want and then meditating on it? Would that help? You know, The Power of Attraction?

READER: Every time you repeat to yourself what you want you are also simultaneously reminding yourself that you don't have it. The real trick is realizing what's in the way of what we want. More often than not we are blocking things from ourselves with our expectations and attitudes.

Maybe this all began for you by trying to gain your Father's acknowledgement? As a child you wanted love and would have done anything, but as an adult you must realize that what your Father denied you only makes it imperative to find it within yourself, not search for another benefactor to reward you. Our happiness is a gift we give ourselves, yet it doesn't have to be like fireworks going off or winning the lottery. Happiness is the middle path where we don't get so euphoric that anything less is a letdown, and we don't get so caught up in our pain that we start to believe our suffering will never end.

A poet once wrote;

"We worship "Yes" and
  Suffer "No", ignoring the
  Question of Balance."

You need to realize saying "no" to someone else's vision of
you is not denying yourself love or happiness. Whatever
you feel your parents denied you was more about their
unawareness than you not being loveable.

MARY: I understand what you're saying, my God it all
seems so clear to hear you say it, but how do I change? I
don't even know the first thing to do!

READER: Of course you do, in fact you've already done
it!

MARY: Really!?

READER: You reached out for help.

MARY: I did?

READER: Sure, you came here.

MARY: I had no idea coming here would turn out like
this!

READER: What did you think was going to happen?
That I would predict you'd meet a tall, dark stranger, or
give you winning lotto numbers?

MARY: Well no…I don't know…I thought you'd tell me
the future.

(The Reader snickers.)

READER: The future must be discovered, not known ahead of time. Anything that can truly change you must necessarily be beyond your current understanding, otherwise you'd know it already and nothing would change. All that has happened here is that I have held up a mirror to reflect the inconsistencies of what you have come to believe about yourself. So now the question is, who are you my dear?

MARY: I'm confused. I know I am a good person but I don't know why no one else seems to see that?

READER: Everyone we've talked about has clearly seen you are a good person, what you aren't understanding is that they have projected their feelings about themselves onto you because they sensed that a good person like you would accept that burden.

MARY: What! Are you saying all the people I've cared about have taken advantage of me? That would mean they didn't love me!

READER: Don't be silly, of course you've been loved; your parents love you, at least as much as they're capable. Not everyone has consciously taken advantage of you either. All I'm saying is that we all go through life generally unaware, like we're sleepwalking, until something wakes us up. We think we love others, we think we understand life, but we're all just stuck in our own thoughts. We worship our likes and dislikes and never suspect that we have our heads buried in the sand of our own ignorance. Everyone justifies their behavior to themselves and blames the world for their victimization. I'm not trying to give you a scapegoat for your unhappiness; I'm trying to help you see the confusion that's keeping you from realizing that you have the power to fix your life by changing how you think about things.

MARY: Are you saying that if I think about things differently then people will treat me differently?

READER: Yes. Let me explain. If you decided to think about your parents differently you might experience who they are in a new way. Then maybe you'd recognize their limitations and feel compassion instead of frustration. You'd see how they have only judged you based on their fears and not on your value as a person. How could they judge you as a person when they hardly know who they are to begin with?

Children don't have to be taught love and trust, that's natural to every child. Fear is what we are taught. We reclaim our natural state of love and trust by dismantling the fear we have been indoctrinated with. Forgive your parents for their ignorance so you can forgive yourself and be free of the prison created by the walls you have built in your own mind.

It is written in the Heart Sutra, "without the walls of the mind and thus without fear...."

Taking down those walls is what I mean by thinking about things differently. If you can do that your Parents will definitely sense a difference in you. Maybe then they would also realize some of their own mistakes and your relations with them will change?

MARY: Oh, wow! ...I so needed to hear this!

READER: Do you see how you have taken on the burdens of others to try and gain love for yourself, when in fact you could only have borne those burdens if your heart was already filled with love? You already possess what you were looking for.

MARY: I wish I could have realized all this before and eliminated the pain I've suffered.

READER: There will always be pain... and love; the most we can learn is non-attachment.

MARY: You mean not being too sentimental?

READER: Not exactly. Non-attachment means not to project your emotions on to things.........."Be careful what you think you want it can only be just what it is."

MARY: I'm not sure I understand.

READER: Nothing we are looking for is in our box of expectations except for disappointment. When we hope for something and then fear we won't get it, we are only imagining something in our mind. The true nature of what we hope to encounter may be much different, therefore to imagine something one way or another ahead of time is really just an illusion. Let the world reveal itself to you. You don't have to make sense of it immediately, just make sure you are brave enough to accept it and then trust that over time you'll figure things out. That way you will always be in harmony with the Tao.

MARY: The Tao?

READER: The Way, The Will of God (He, She, or It).

MARY: I feel overwhelmed.

READER: You're doing fine.

MARY: This is like therapy.

READER: I have a few Therapists as clients. What we're doing now is more concentrated than their usual process, however, no one gets any closer to enlightenment than the natural flow of their evolution will allow.

MARY: What do you mean?

READER: I can tell you stuff and you can understand me intellectually, but nothing is going to really transform in your life without you doing the work and struggling through the experiences we have been talking about. You have to come to feel the truth of what I'm suggesting not just consider it as an idea. If it were that simple no one would ever be unhappy.

MARY: Is it natural for enlightenment to make you feel depressed?

READER: Enlightenment doesn't eliminate what you don't like about life; rather it requires you to clearly see and accept that the perfection of the Universe is a result of everything in it (both good and bad) fitting together harmoniously. Our notions of perfection are really more about prejudice, control, and limitation.

MARY: I suppose you're right.

READER: Let's work with the Tarot now. I usually like to save the cards for the end of the reading as a sort of summary to make sure I've touched on everything that's important.

(At this point The Reader reaches for the black velvet bag on the table and removes a pack of well-worn cards.)

Right now I'd like you to close your eyes and think about everything we've just spoken about. Take a moment to search within yourself for the strong, fully evolved woman that represents who you will be once some of these new perspectives we've discussed have taken hold… She's in there somewhere, if you can't find her right now then at least call for her………..While your eyes are closed I'm going to hold the cards in front of your throat.

(For several seconds The Reader holds the cards in front of Mary's throat while the young woman sits and breathes quietly with her eyes closed. He then begins to shuffle the deck as Mary continues to sit quietly with her eyes shut. After both shuffling and cutting the deck 3 times The Reader then lays out 7 cards in a pattern that looks like the letter "H".)

You can open your eyes now.

MARY: Why did you hold the cards over my throat?

READER: In the Qabalistic Tradition the area over the throat is known as DaaTh or "Knowledge". It's the place where our lessons, or the enlightenment we have yet to discover is waiting. In the Rosicrucian Tradition that same area is referred to as, "The Abyss", or the dark place within us that must be crossed to connect the "Beauty" of the Heart with the "Crown" at the top of the head where our Higher Self resides.

MARY: Oh, that's interesting. I only asked because I had always heard that the person getting the reading is supposed to shuffle the cards.

READER: Some people like to do it that way. I think it's energetically more effective if I hold the cards and tap directly into the Knowledge Center that I just mentioned without the person's conscious anxiety getting in the way.

MARY: I get it, so what do the cards say?

READER: The three cards on the left represent the present, the one in the middle is the transition, and the three cards on the right are the possibilities for the future. Five of these seven cards are from The Major Arcana and represent forces greater than you or I at work.

MARY: The Major what?

READER: The 78 cards of the Tarot are divided into two sections. The first is called the Major Arcana and consists of 22 "Trump Cards" that represent the Spiritual or Archetypal energies of the deck. The second section is the Minor Arcana, which contains 56 cards divided into 4 suits- Wands, Cups, Swords, and Pentacles. Each of these suits is then numbered from 1 to 10 with 4 additional Court Cards (Kings, Queens, Knights, and Pages). The Minor Arcana represents the more mundane aspects of any matter as well as the things that are directly under our control.

Because there are 5 Trumps here it indicates to me that you have arrived at an inevitable crossroads in your life and the time has come for an important lesson or realization. This is good news in so far as you chose to come here and embrace this change, which means you are in harmony with the flow of events.

MARY: I can assure you that when I came here I had no idea that anything like what we've talked about was going to happen.

READER: On the contrary, the part of you that truly "knows" was quite aware of what you were walking into.

MARY: (Smiling modestly) If you say so……….

READER: Looking at the 3 cards signifying the present, the first one that catches my attention is The Moon, a Major Arcana Card that's symbolic of one's inner landscape or the subconscious. In some instances this card can also signify voluntary change. It needs to be kept in mind though that any changes we might be speaking of will probably entail having to face some sort of inner fear. The lobster crawling out of the pool at the bottom of the image represents this fear in its most primal aspects.

The card above The Moon is the 8 of Swords and below it is another Major Arcana card titled "Strength." The suit of Swords is about our thought processes and the 8 of Swords shows a woman tied up and surrounded by a fence of swords. This is symbolic of being tied up by our own ideas. The Strength card refers to inner fortitude and the ability to master our obsessions and lower drives. All in all I'd say these first three cards signifying inner change, escaping false ideas, and self-mastery are a pretty concise summary of what we've been talking about and a clear picture of what is currently confronting you.

MARY: The pictures are pretty evocative. The one of the lady tied up makes me feel stupid, but the other one of the woman with the lion gives me a better feeling.

READER: That's good, but what about the one in the middle?

MARY: The Moon?

READER: Yes

MARY: That one is kind of creepy. There is a vague, almost mysterious quality to it that feels like I don't quite know what's going on. It makes me uneasy.

READER: The Moon is symbolic of our emotions and since you came here in a state of emotional confusion it is effectively acting as a mirror of your current mood.

MARY: That makes sense.

READER: The middle card in the overall spread signifies the transition from present to future and in this case it is the Page of Wands. I think this refers to the courage to express your desires, something you have been reticent to do in the past and this has caused you problems.

MARY: I don't want to be so willing to please someone anymore until I see the other person is interested in who I am…and what I want.

READER: Well then the 3 cards for the future are quite a group for you. The Devil, Death, and The Sun, all Major Arcana cards… Wow!

MARY: Is that good or bad, because two of those cards look pretty scary.

READER: Try not to look at them literally. The Devil is about overcoming the blockages within us and Death refers to inevitable change.

MARY: I don't know. My friend went to one of those Gypsy Psychics and some of those cards came up and the woman told her she was cursed. After that, the woman wanted a lot of money to remove the curse. She told my friend someone had put the evil eye on her or something like that. She also said my friend would find her Soul Mate but then that person would be taken away from her by the person who cursed her.

READER: Unfortunately you're friend went to see a con woman and not a psychic. Did she pay?

MARY: Of course not, the Woman wanted like $1500; but some of the stuff she told my friend was true.

READER: I'm sure it was, but that's not because the woman was necessarily psychic. You see, we're not all as unique as we'd like to think and that's simply because everyone basically desires and fears the same things. Once you find out what someone is specifically frightened of it's not hard to then manipulate him or her into feeling a lot worse so that they will be open to believing the stupidest nonsense. Add to that a New Age Buzz Word like "Soul Mate" that's easily misinterpreted and the scene is set for the "mark" to be conned. It's good your friend didn't pay.

MARY: She couldn't afford to, but now she's freaked out by what the woman said and worries if she's cursed. By the way, what did you mean when you referred to a Soul Mate as a New Age Buzzword?

READERr: The popular notion of a Soul Mate is like Cinderella and Prince Charming living happily ever after. That image makes money for both Psychics and Hollywood, but the reality of a Soul Mate is that they're someone who is necessary for you to meet in terms of your personal evolution; and that can be either happy or tragic depending on what you need to learn.

MARY: Interesting.

READER: And for the record, I can assure you your friend is not cursed. Now let's continue our conversation and don't worry, there will be no additional fee here beyond what you paid before sitting down.

MARY: I didn't think there would be. Hey, maybe my friend should come and see you?

READER: I only take Clients by referral, so it would be up to you to tell her. Also, she has to want to come of her own free will; don't try to force her, even if you think it's the right thing.

MARY: Oh no, I wouldn't do that. I think she'll want to come, I mean, this is amazing!

READER: Thank you. Now let's get back to the cards and see what the future might hold.

In the image for The Devil we see two people chained to the perch upon which the Demon sits. The chains on these people's necks are very loose, which means they can choose to remove their shackles and walk away. We all have that choice when it comes to many of the obstacles in our lives, so what will you do? The Death Card signifies inevitable change and The Sun is freedom and liberation. In short I think the Tarot is saying the time for change has come. You can initiate this change or it can happen to you like a brick falling out of the sky and hitting you in the head, but change is inevitable. A part of you is ready for this because you found your way here. What remains to be seen though is if you are going to do anything different when you leave here? I think The Sun card is a strong indicator that you will and all of this will work out for the best.

MARY: I don't know…. I hope so.

READER: I think the cards have verified most of what we have been discussing, all that remains now is if you have any questions?

(At this point all the stage lights go out except for a pair of spotlights, one focused on The Reader and the other on Mary. During the time the room is in darkness The Reader sits and silently contemplates the cards on the table, while Mary seems very anxious and almost panicked, as if the light has only disappeared for her. When the stage lights come back on a few seconds later Mary appears to have regained her composure somewhat, although for the remainder of the scene her manner is that of someone who seems quite anxious about something.)

MARY: I know this is probably going to sound stupid, but will anyone ever love me enough to want to marry me and have children?

READER: Do you want to have children?

MARY: Yes, I think so.

READER: Then you may not like what I'm going to say.

MARY: What?

READER: If it's meant for you to have kids you will and if it's not, you won't.

MARY: But if you're Psychic aren't you supposed to know if I will or not?

READER: What I do know is that without a better sense of self you can't really have a good relationship, and without a loving relationship any children you bring into this world will be at a disadvantage and probably give someone like me more business in the future. Don't be in a rush to perpetuate the same sort of mistakes that brought you to see me. You have some very important issues in front of you right now and I suggest you confront them head on instead of asking for assurances about things that are not realistic for you at this time.

MARY: I know what you're saying is true, but I look around and see all my friends pairing up and my cousin who is my age just had her second child. My Mother keeps saying she's afraid I'll be an old maid. I feel under a lot of pressure.

READER: All these Major Arcana cards you have here are to let you know you have reached a very important crossroads in your life. Your destiny will be determined by deciding for yourself what you want to believe, the laws of the Universe or the laws of society. The laws of the Universe are offering you a gift of awareness and freedom. The laws of society brought you here in frustration and dissatisfaction. Make your choice, but I think you're going to have a hard time going along as you have been. My advice? Accept what you're being shown and be reborn in an ocean of new awareness.

MARY: What does that even mean? What new awareness? If everyone else believes life is a certain way then what does seeing things differently amount too? More frustration? I don't mean to sound so negative after all you've said, but I don't know anyone who really lives the way you're talking about. Everyone just wants to have money and things and be loved. If we're all after the same things wouldn't it be better to stick with the crowd and increase our chances of getting the normal things in life? The things we all want.

READER: I am not here to tell you what to believe, but there is a thing called truth.

MARY: What is the truth? Tell me what that is and I'll follow it.

READER: No one can tell you the truth. What we have been talking about here concerns discovering it for yourself as opposed to following a menu established by someone else. Your men have believed the truth consists of you giving and them taking, yet that leaves you drained and bitter. If you try for something different and it turns out to be better, then you have discovered a new truth for yourself. You are at that crossroads now, my dear. You must contemplate which path you will take.

(A long moment of silence passes as The Reader and Mary look into each other's eyes. Suddenly, an alarm goes off (the theme from the television show "X Files") and The Reader removes a cell phone from the bookcase and shuts off the alarm.)

READER: Unfortunately we're out of time.

MARY: So you can't tell me if I'll meet anyone?

READER: You're young and attractive; of course you'll meet someone.

MARY: I apologize for being so silly after all you've told me. I really do appreciate the things you've said, but there is a part of me that still feels hopeless.

READER: If Love is the most valuable thing in the world then it should have a high price and that cost will be different for everyone. For you it means learning how to sit in the vacuum of yourself and breathe. I'm sorry if that sounds like too much, but it's what you need to learn. Each of us must come to appreciate ourselves before we can truly love others. You have reached the limits of pretending otherwise because now you know better. Once you get a glimpse of the truth you must live it, if you don't then life will hold nothing for you that really matters. Trust me dear, you are in a great position. Have the courage to do what your heart is showing you. Now, if you don't have any further questions, we're done.

MARY: (Sighing) You're right, I'll probably be okay. Thank you. By the way when would you recommend I come and see you again?

READER: When you have something different to talk about. Maybe after you've created some of the changes we've discussed there will be some new challenges for us to look at?

MARY: I get it. Thank you very much for your help.

READER: My pleasure.

(Both The Reader and Mary stand and then walk

together toward the entrance. When they arrive at the curtain The Reader holds it open and Mary exits, after which he follows her out.

Curtain

THE SECOND READING

CHARACTERS

The Reader

Same as in the First Reading

The Client (Tom)

A handsome, "Arty" looking young man in his thirties

Scene

The room looks exactly the same as in the first reading, except now The Reader is seated alone at the table and sipping a mug of tea. He is wearing the same clothes, so it should be assumed that it is later on the same day.

After a few moments, The Reader puts down his mug and reaches to remove a book from the bookcase. He opens the book to a marked page and begins to read aloud;

"Thirty spokes are joined together in a wheel,
but it is the center hole
that allows the wheel to function.

We mold clay into a pot,
but it is the emptiness inside
that makes the vessel useful.

We fashion wood for a house,
but it is the emptiness inside
that makes it livable.

We work with the substantial,
but the emptiness is what we use."

When he finishes reading, The Reader puts the book down on the table and stares off into space for a while until the sound of his phone alarm going off breaks the silence. He turns off the alarm, puts the book back in the bookcase, and then heads across the room and exits through the large burgundy curtain.

A moment later The Reader re-enters the room and holds the curtain open for The Client who follows him in. After directing The Client to which chair he should sit in, The Reader then sits down and they begin talking.

READER: Okay Tom, what would you like to know?

TOM: I'm interested in anything that'll contribute to my enlightenment.

READER: Hmmm, what exactly do you mean by that?

TOM: What did you mean by, "What would I like to know?"

READER: Well…people usually come for a reading when something isn't working out for them. If everything was going fine why would they need to talk to someone like me? Like the saying goes, "If it ain't broke, don't fix it." So…is there anything you'd like to see working better in your life?

TOM: Fair enough. Let me think…

(Several moments of silence ensue as Tom furrows his brow and stares down at the reading table. The Reader watches him for a few seconds and then breaks the silence with a question.)

READER: What do you do?

TOM: I'm a musician.

READER: Professionally?

TOM: Not exactly.

READER: Oh?

TOM: Well, I'm in a band, but we're not working right now.

READER: So what do you do to earn a living?

TOM: I'm a bartender.

READER: How's that going?

TOM: It pays the bills but I'm pretty frustrated with it.

READER: When was the last time your band played a gig?

TOM: About 6 months ago.

READER: Why is that?

TOM: I don't know, it seems like it's hard for us to agree on anything.

READER: Are you in a relationship?

TOM: I don't know.

READER: You don't know?

TOM: Well, there's this chick I've been seeing... but, I don't know...

READER: Is there anything right now working out the way you'd like?

TOM: Sure.

READER: What would that be?

TOM: My Spiritual Studies are going well.

READER: Really? What are you studying?

TOM: I've been reading about developing my Psychic Abilities, Remote viewing, stuff like that.

READER: Where are you getting your information?

TOM: From an Internet blog by a guy named Beelzebuddy.

READER: Do you find these studies are useful in regards to the other stuff in your life that isn't working?

TOM: What do you mean?

(The Reader tilts his head like a dog when it's confused and then reaches over and grabs one of the large books on the table.)

READER: Let's get to work. What's your birthday?

TOM: September 1, 1980

(The Reader opens the book and flips through the pages until he finds what he's looking for. After studying the information in front of him for a few moments he then begins speaking)

READER: Do you know if you were born before or after 12 noon?

TOM: I'm not sure.

READER: All right, don't guess. Just answer me this... How curious are you, or better yet, how distracted can you get?

TOM: Well, I am interested in a lot of things.

READER: How often do you finish what you start?

TOM: There are some things that I let slide, but then again I can also be pretty responsible….

READER: …..When you have to be, right?

TOM: I guess you could say that.

READER: Have the responsibilities at your job caused you to let your music slide?

TOM: It's not like I'm obsessed with my job or anything like that. I plan on getting back to playing; it's just that I've gotten really interested in Psychic stuff.

READER: So let me get this straight… you're working at a job you don't like, reading about Psychic stuff, and also thinking about getting back to your music?…. I would say you have a Gemini Moon.

TOM: I thought I was a Virgo?

READER: Your Sun is in Virgo, but you Moon is in Gemini. To say you are a Virgo is like saying you're a man; there were 9 other planets circling in the heavens on the day you were born and each of them represents an archetypal aspect of your character. For instance, Saturn would represent your control issues, Neptune your imagination, the Moon your emotional style, and so on.

(The Reader takes the next few moments to look at the book again before continuing to speak)

You have a Virgo Sun and it squares a Gemini Moon. Both of these signs are ruled by Mercury, which represents communication and information. As a result, you feel an emotional need to have a constantly changing set of circumstances (your Gemini Moon), which you are forever juggling and trying to orchestrate together into some useful pattern (your Virgo Sun).

(Tom leans forward in his seat and stares intently at the reader)

You also have Mars in Scorpio, which is always about power, and that both sextiles your Sun and inconjuncts your Moon. In short these configurations can cause you to oscillate significantly back and forth between ambition and withdrawal, as well as lending a stealth air to how you generally deal with people. In other words, you don't like people to know what you're up to and usually keep things on the down low.

TOM: It says all that in the book?

READER: Not necessarily, that's my interpretation.... any questions?

TOM: Not bad

READER: You also have Mercury and Jupiter conjunct in Virgo squaring Neptune in Sagittarius. This aspect could cause you to either get distracted in details and lose sight of the big picture or else avoid details and then not finish a lot of what you start. With the proper effort though this could also be a very creative aspect and make you someone who is able to turn an inspiration into a piece of writing or music.

Another aspect I'm noticing is Venus in Cancer trine Uranus in Scorpio, with Saturn in Virgo as their midpoint. On one hand this could give you some real control issues and make you more than a little manipulative or, on the higher side, it could also make you someone who can successfully direct a group toward a common goal.

The last major line-up I'm seeing is a square between Venus in Cancer and Pluto in Libra. Like the other aspects I've mentioned, this one holds a great deal of creative potential but it can also be a very passionate or even quite angry influence, especially in interactions with women or, dare I say, parents.

TOM: If all that you're saying is true, then I'm a walking contradiction who is equal parts good and bad. Couldn't you say that about everybody? And then all this control stuff you're talking about-aren't we all, more or less, trying to control each other?

READER: Astrological aspects don't determine your life, your choices do. Many people have conflicting aspects in their charts; that just means the responsibility is ultimately on the individual to make a choice about their evolution.

As far as control issues go, maybe I need to clarify. There are essentially two types of control; either you try to control others, or you resist letting anyone control you. There are also two essential styles of control. One type is to go into a crowded room and try to dominate the scene and the other is to find an empty room so there is no risk of anyone dominating you. The thing is that both of these approaches are ultimately about giving your power away and accomplish similar ends; kind of a paradox, don't you think?

And lastly, to answer your question about everyone trying to control everyone else, needing to control people is usually fear based and the chickens always come home to roost on that one.

TOM: What do you mean?

READER: Those who feel the need to be in control are rarely able to see how they are actually the ones being controlled by circumstances.

TOM: (Nervously scratching the side of his head) This isn't exactly what I wanted to talk about when I decided to come here.

READER: Okay, then what would you like to talk about?

TOM: I came here for Esoteric Knowledge, you know, The Mysteries, that kind of stuff, and I figured that someone who does what you do would be able to let me in on some real info.

(The Reader leans back in his chair and casually observes Tom)

READER: Sure, what would you like to know?

TOM: Are the Illuminati real?

READER: Where did you hear of the Illuminati?

TOM: That Spiritual Master I mentioned named Beelzebuddy writes about them on his website.

READER: He's a Spiritual Master?

TOM: Yeah. He say's the Illuminati are manipulating the mass consciousness on the planet in order to prevent those of us who are capable of ascending to the next Ray of awareness from gaining our enlightenment.

READER: That sounds interesting, however, I think the late Robert Anton Wilson made up the term "Illuminati" in his Sci-fi books.

(The Reader leans forward in his chair and rests his elbows on the table.)

At any rate, let's get back to Astrology for a moment. As we speak transiting Pluto is in trine to your natal conjunction of Mercury and Jupiter, which would represent the unveiling of secrets. At the same time, transiting Neptune is squaring your Moon and opposing your Sun and that would refer to illusions. One distinct difficulty for you at this time is figuring out the right things to pay attention to.

TOM: I don't understand.

(The Reader now resumes leaning back in his chair before continuing.)

READER: Well consider this, if the Illuminati actually existed they are so above our pay grade why worry? On the other hand, this woman you're seeing but not seeing might offer some real food for insight regarding your actual evolution. That is if you can be honest with yourself about what you're holding back from her and why. Another interesting question might be why you're still in a band that doesn't play together anymore? If that's the case are you really in a band?

TOM: Is it that you can't tell me about the Illuminati because you're initiated and sworn to secrecy?

READER: Do you not want to talk about anything real in your life because you're sworn to secrecy?

(At this point Tom starts to laugh nervously while The Reader just looks at him.)

TOM: Okay, okay, you're right............I feel stuck in a rut and I don't know what to do.........I don't know why I haven't looked for some new dudes to play music with... maybe I'm wondering if I really want to play anymore? And this chick I do an occasional booty call with, well, she's willing to hang around so I figure why not? I haven't promised her anything so technically how could anyone get hurt?

READER: Sure, she can split whenever she wants...No harm, no foul, right?

TOM: Yeah

READER: You know people hurting others is not a technical matter, being hurt is actual and it's based on what we do, as well what we withhold from others. It sounds like you're trying to avoid life by engaging in speculative realities, like Illuminati conspiracies, when your actual life is right there in your face with all its inescapable confusion.... So... with that in mind, what would you like to talk about with the remainder of our time? It's up to you.

TOM: I don't know. What can be done? Can you fix anything for me? If not, what's the point?

READER: The point is what kind of life do you want and how can you start creating it instead of letting it create you?

TOM: In his blog Beelzebuddy say's that only an Adept Magician can create a real life in the face of the Illuminati's negative entropy.

READER: How can anybody argue with that?

TOM: So you agree with Beelzebuddy?

READER: It's not about talking the talk, but walking the walk. If your Guru offers a way, try it, if it doesn't work, move on. Has Beelzebuddy offered any tangible things you can try in order to liberate yourself?

TOM: He has a book that he's written and he offers it for sale on his website. It's called "The Sirius Way to Mastery".

READER: He is undoubtedly a Sirius Dude...

.

TOM: He's referring to the constellation Sirius in outer space.

READER: I know. He also sounds like one of those info-mercial guys that sell books on how to make millions flipping real estate properties; for Ten Dollars everyone can be independently wealthy.

TOM: Do you have a better book to sell me for my "liberation"?

READER: I have published some books, but I'm not hustling them here, let's stay on point.

First, you need to acknowledge what you're doing or not doing in pursuit of your dreams and in your association with the young woman you mentioned. Next, accept responsibility for how your actions are making you feel. Once you determine how you feel then do something about it. Give up music or start practicing; open up your heart to the girl or stop seeing her, it's your choice.

TOM: No need to get so intense, dude....

READER: Sorry, I just think it's a waste of your money to talk about the Illuminati with me when we could be talking about your personal Illumination. A real Adept once said, "Magick is the Science and Art of causing Change to occur in conformity with Will." In other words, the Magick your Beelzebuddy talks about is really nothing more than experimenting with thought and action until your desires and attainments are in harmony with the world around you.

TOM: In harmony with the world around, do you mean conforming to what everyone else is doing?

READER: Not in the way you're suggesting. The positive, the negative, the good, the bad, they're all necessary. A criminal and a policeman are both in harmony with the world if each is following what they truly believe. The outcome of their respective choices and subsequent actions will eventually become apparent, yet no matter what happens more choices will be necessary and more responsibilities will accrue. It's this organic dynamic that constitutes freedom and makes the world a perfect classroom with endless lessons to learn.

TOM: But wouldn't all of that still happen even if I did nothing?

READER: Exactly!

TOM: So what is the reason for me to do anything? Why bother?

READER: Because you never know what you might discover.

TOM: But if it doesn't matter…?

READER: All evolution matters because life exists to perpetuate itself …it's partially your choice and partially a confluence of forces… that's all you really need to concern yourself with. But even if you abdicate your power to choose, that is still a choice……

TOM: But then…

(At this point The Reader interrupts Tom.)

READER: I'm sorry to cut you off, but we need to change direction here and start to unravel some of what's driving you to detach from dealing with what is actually happening in your life….If that's okay?

TOM: I'm not detached. Don't you think I worry about this shit all the time?

READER: What do you call it when you worry about something all the time but don't do anything about it?

TOM: Being stuck?

READER: Bingo! Now, what do you call it when you

choose to focus on something that really doesn't matter instead of addressing how you're stuck and what you need to do about it?

TOM: Denial?

READER: We're really making up for lost time here. Let me ask you this, Do you like to play music?

TOM: Hell yes, I used to love it!

READER: Why did you stop loving it?

TOM: I told you the band I'm in is on hiatus and I'm not feeling inspired.

READER: You have to love to play to be able to play well. You can only be in a real band if you play well. It goes love, play well, band; without the love to begin with, you're nowhere. Why don't you just begin by falling in love with playing again? Play along with records you like, learn some solo pieces, try to write some songs. Wouldn't that make you happy again? You began by telling me you wanted to know anything that would contribute to your enlightenment, well I'm suggesting if you start to seriously play music again your perspective on things might change toward a more enlightened one. Don't underestimate the power of the creative energy coming from you to attract something new into your sphere. Maybe after you start to play again you'll eventually get really excited about a new song you've learned (or maybe even written!) and that energy will lead to an unexpected meeting and new people to play with?

TOM: Yeah, that sounds fair.

READER: Now what about this girl you've mentioned? What's your hesitancy about there? Is she cute? Does she seem like a good person?

TOM: I don't know if it's about her. I think it's more that I'm not ready for any kind of commitment.

READER: What does that mean… commitment to what, exactly?

TOM: You know what chicks want, that whole monogamy thing leading to living together, marriage, and planning your whole life.

READER: Are you seeing this person for who they really are or as a stereotype to justify something to yourself?

TOM: Justify what?

READER: Perhaps your aversion to responsibility? If you show her you like her then you'll have to be responsible for those feelings…maybe you're the manipulative one, not her? By the way, what is this young lady's first initial?

TOM: Huh?

READER: The first initial of her first name.

TOM: M

(The Reader takes a deep breath and then begins his unique hand movements while Tom watches him with a perplexed look. After finishing with his little ritual, The Reader then sits silently for a moment before speaking.)

READER: This girl has a lot going for her, but she

doesn't think she does. That's why she's willing to play the games of a cliché "chick" and accept the games of a cliché man in return. The reality is that neither of you have the courage to simply be who you are and see what happens. You're assuming what a stereotype wants and penalizing a real person for your miscalculation. You want to believe she's nothing but a manipulative "chic" because being emotionally responsible to anyone scares the crap out of you. She's a giver so you could just take advantage of her and not give anything in return; in fact she's already letting you do that.

TOM: Hey, I didn't ask her to do anything; she made her own choices.

READER: Yeah, right. You know some people believe that if they intentionally withhold information it's technically not lying. After all they didn't say anything that wasn't true. So we're back to the technicalities you mentioned earlier.

TOM: But I've done nothing wrong, right?

READER: Perhaps, but what does that kind of logic do for you?

TOM: What do you mean?

READER: You see my theory on why people get together is that each person holds the key to the other's lessons. You need to open up so you can give and she needs to open up so she can receive. Both of you have confidence and fear issues around the opening up; she needs to believe she deserves love without having to try so hard, and you need to risk that someone will take the love you offer and not reject you.

(Tom sits for several seconds in a stunned silence.)

TOM: Shit, I feel.......... Naked.

READER: So go home and try to write a song about it and see what happens.

TOM: Yeah, right...Whoa, I mean how do you know this shit? Now that you've said it, that's exactly what's going on. This is insane.

READER: I have my moments. However, the question is, how did you get into such a spy versus spy place in your dealings with women? We need to talk about that.

TOM: Okay?

READER: Do you get along with your parents?

TOM: Better now with my Mom, but my Dad and I have never seen eye to eye.

READER: Are they both still alive?

TOM: Yes

READER: Are they still together?

TOM: Technically.

READER: Technicalities again, what's your Dad's first initial?

TOM: T

READER: Are you named after him?

TOM: Yeah

(The Reader goes into his silent place and works his hands like he has before.)

READER: Your Dad is pretty tightly wound, like one of those old, leather covered books with a little padlock on it.

TOM: You got that right.

READER: You felt judged by him from pretty early on and you were, but what you don't realize is a lot of it was projection. In other words, he took a break from criticizing himself to criticize you. Believe it or not, you actually frighten him a little.

TOM: Are you kidding?

READER: No. What does he do?

TOM: He's a Cop.

READER: Interesting.

TOM: Meaning?

READER: You're sensitivity makes your Father feel a real need to assert his assumptions about what it means to be "manly". He loves you. He just doesn't know how to open up and show it. He thinks it's weak to be sensitive and if you're sensitive then he feels he needs to toughen you up. Your resentment of that makes him seem like a failure as a Father and that makes him feel angry, and weak. It's a vicious circle that goes round and round.

(Tom's eyes go blank and he looks off to the side.)

The tragedy here, if there is one, is that you have tried to be as insensitive as he is in hope of gaining his approval.

(The Reader's comment manages to snap Tom back from his reverie and the young man replies belligerently....)

TOM: No way man, I've rebelled against him since I was in High School!

READER: That's right, and how did you act out your rebellion? Like you didn't care, when in fact your heart was breaking and you hated yourself for feeling unlovable. You became your own enemy. It's time you started being your true self. You have projected your shit with your Dad into your whole life, so now on the outside you're the strong, unemotional one who is dying inside because you have created such high walls between you and everything your heart longs for.

(Tom stares blankly at The Reader)

Maybe that's why you can't let your lady friend in?

(Tom continues staring)

Now tell me your Mom's first Initial?

TOM: Huh?.......... oh, M.

(The Reader works his hands and then reflects for a few moments before continuing.)

READER: Your Mom tried for years to be a go between for you and your Dad, but she's too invested in trying to please him to really stand up for you. She was always hoping you would just adjust like she did. You're getting along with her better now because she's seeing your Father get old and realizing she should have done things a little differently with you.

TOM: I think you're right. Sometimes I feel sorry for her. I try to be nicer than he was. It's hard though because she gets all weepy and then I start to get emotional and then I've got to get out of there. I don't know what to do…

READER: Now we're getting somewhere… maybe this girl you're seeing is like your Mom and you don't know what to do with her either?

(A long moment of silence ensues as Tom stares into space and The Reader watches him)

We don't have much time left, so let's finish up working with the Tarot.

(The Reader reaches over and grabs the black velvet bag on the table)

I like to save the cards for the end to check that I've covered everything you need, and also because sometimes the cards can offer insights on what you might do next.

TOM: Cool…. By the way, what are those movements you do with your hands after I tell you a person's first initial?

READER: It's a technique known as "Remote Muscle Testing". It's often used by Alternative Health Care Professionals to test the body's energetic sensitivity to certain foods or nutrients. I use it to test the environment within an individual's Chakras in order to get a read on the core energy driving their behavior.

TOM: Awesome…I've read about the Chakras in Beelzebuddy's blog. You must be pretty psychic.

(The Reader removes the cards and starts to explain to Tom what will happen next.)

READER: I want you to begin by putting your hands flat on the table and closing your eyes.

(Tom adjusts himself in his chair and then complies with the Reader's request)

Now try and bring to mind an image of yourself, like you are looking in a mirror and can see your reflection. Next, imagine that there is a zipper on the top of your head and you can pull this zipper down the front of your face and the front of your body so that this image of yourself you have been looking at can be removed like an overcoat. What's underneath? You don't have to tell me, just consider it…… Imagine this is your evolved self you're looking at. Does the person you see seem confident or frightened, happy or sad? Look into their eyes. Step closer toward them. Reach out and try to take their hand. Are they reaching out to you as well? Consciously open yourself to a communion with your future being, and while you do that I'm going to hold the cards in front of you for a few moments.

(At this point The Reader goes into his own meditative place as he holds the cards in front of Tom's throat. After several moments he begins to shuffle the deck and cut it 3 times. Once he has laid out the cards, The Reader resumes speaking to Tom.)

You can open your eyes now. Of the 7 cards you see here, the 3 on the left represent the present state of affairs, the one in the center describes the transition, and the 3 on the right show the possibilities for the future.

The top card on the left is the King of Swords, which represents a restricting influence in your life, and in this case I feel it is symbolic of your Father.

The bottom card on the left is the 7 of Swords. This is always a tricky card to interpret because it's hard to know what the character in it is doing; is he stealing away with the swords or smuggling them in? I feel this card represents your dishonesty with yourself and, as a result, the suspicions you have of others.

The middle card of the three is the Major Arcana card titled "Temperance". In this card we see an angel pouring water back and forth between a pair of cups he holds in his right and left hands. This signifies a need to balance one's emotions. It is also important to notice that the water flowing back and forth between the cups is defying gravity. Water pours straight down, yet in this image the liquid is literally flying straight across from one cup to the other. What does this mean? Are you manufacturing emotions that are not real to your situation or are you denying what you feel? For example, are you suppressing your feelings so it seems as though you don't care, when in fact you care very deeply? Are you pretending you are strong and self-sufficient when in fact you are feeling vulnerable and insecure? Are your expectations and worries causing you to have emotions before anything has happened to be emotional about?

If we now combine the meanings of these 3 cards together, it becomes clear that it's necessary for you to re-examine your emotions in order to see the difference between who you learned to be in the past and who you are now.

TOM: You're completely right about my mistrust of others, but is that really because I don't trust myself?

READER: Let's talk about the young woman you've mentioned. If you can see she feels something for you and yet you're holding back from her what do you think that means?

TOM: You have a point. But I don't think of myself as a dishonest person out to take advantage of anyone.

READER: Most people don't think of themselves that way, but the selfishness out there in the world is undeniable. So what is it that creates the disconnection between what we intend to do as opposed to what we actually do?

TOM: I would guess it's basically fear.

READER: I think you're right, so what are you afraid of?

TOM: That I will be rejected.

READER: So you do the rejecting first?

TOM: But it doesn't feel like I'm doing that. I'm just being careful so I don't make a fool out of myself and get hurt.

READER: Be careful you're not giving your power away by suggesting something to yourself that becomes a self-fulfilling prophecy.

TOM: No doubt.

READER: Let's move on with the cards.

The card in the transition position is the Major Arcana image known as "The Tower." This is probably one of the most feared cards in the deck along with Death and The Devil. The destruction going on in the image looks scary, but in essence it is an illustration of enlightenment. The Tower itself represents belief structures in our lives that have become outdated. The lightning bolt from above striking the crown at the top of the Tower symbolizes an epiphany, while the flames and people being cast out are the things in our lives that must naturally fall away once we have come to know better. Ultimately The Tower symbolizes a necessary upheaval that will ultimately lead us to our evolution.

TOM: Do I have a choice about this or is it going to happen anyway?

READER: Of course it's up to you.

TOM: Well it sure doesn't feel like it.

READER: Why?

TOM: If I don't want something to happen and yet it happens anyway how can you say I wanted it?

READER: If we feel strong enough about something to actively deny it, then we are giving our power away to it....did you ever notice how dogs are drawn to people who are afraid of them....

TOM: That's true, although I usually feel more

comfortable choosing my poison as opposed to being poisoned.

READER: It's ironic for you to say that, particularly in light of how we have worked out that many of your current emotional choices are based on the relationship you've had with your Father. When you react to a current situation based on subconscious programing from the past then I would hardly call that "choosing" in the sense you're implying.

TOM: Well since we are all so tied up with one another does anyone ever really make their own choices? Isn't everything we do relative?

READER: In this case are we talking about relative to you or your Father's perspective?

TOM: Explain that.

READER: You've been basing all your reactions to life as if you were dealing with your Father...are you ready to create life from your own point of view based on what is actually happening to you at any given moment? Are you ready to live your truth and not react to your sense memories of your Dad?

TOM: But what is the truth? What is real?

READER: That has to be discovered by trying something different and facing the consequences. Let's keep going with the cards and see what possibilities the future holds.

In the top position on the right is the Major Arcana card known as "The Moon". This card is symbolic of the world of Dreams or the "Astral Plane." It's what the Qabalist's refer to as The World of Foundation and represents our inner landscape where ideas exist before they manifest materially into what we commonly think of as reality. Because this card symbolizes the thoughts that precede action, it is also indicative of voluntary change, or the conscious participation in what is happening to us that must be part of our natural evolutionary cycles. The mysterious and haunting quality of the landscape depicted in this card further signifies that the changes represented by this image can often include more than a little fear and trepidation as one is forced to confront what Psychologists refer to as "The Shadow Self."

The middle card on the right is the 5 of Pentacles and shows a pair of unfortunate beggars in a snowstorm passing underneath the stained glass window of a church. When this card was originally drawn at the beginning of the 20th Century, poor folk like those depicted in the picture could have gone into a church to find shelter from the storm. The beggars in this image though are so caught up in their suffering they are not even aware of the church. As a result, the card implies the need to not only deal with whatever the current situation may be, but also, in a greater sense, to understand its purpose in relation to our overall evolution.

What are you not recognizing about your current circumstances? Could it be your present difficulties are the seeds of your future liberation?

The bottom card is the 3 of Wands and that's about new creative possibilities approaching.

TOM: What do you mean, new creative possibilities?

READER: Perhaps if you get back to playing your music

something new may develop there….or maybe if you give that girl a chance you'll be glad you did…… true creativity is about both life and art….at any rate, I don't predict the future I'm just trying to prepare you for it.

"(A period of silence ensues, during which time The Reader and Tom meditate quietly over the cards spread out on the table. While both men are deep in contemplation the sound of a Raven calling can be heard faintly in the distance. When the voice of the bird starts to grow progressively louder, The Reader looks up from the cards to watch Tom, as the younger man begins glancing around and reacting as though he's not sure if what he is hearing is real or not.

"Once the screeching finally reaches a deafening crescendo, the calling of the bird suddenly starts to rapidly fade away until eventually the stage is quiet once again and the Reader and Tom are now looking into each others eyes.)

READER: Do you have any questions?

TOM: Yeah, uh, where do you get this stuff? It's pretty amazing what you know… I mean do you hear voices, or see spirits, or what?

READER: If you mean, "hear" like I'm hearing you speak, or "see" like I'm looking at you, not necessarily. We all have intuition and at times that can seem like a voice or a vision, but usually it's more like a thought inside my head that the rest of me knows to give my full attention to…. Do you ever hear or see things?

TOM: I don't know. Sometimes it's hard to tell what's real.

READER: We've talked about a lot of things today that you thought were real, maybe now you're not so sure? And maybe some of the things you felt couldn't be real now seem like they could be?

TOM: I don't know what I feel right now. I just want to get past my confusion. I feel so pressured.

READER: What's pressuring you?

TOM: What I want seems simple enough but then it gets complicated when other people's interests get involved. I can't help worrying what other people are expecting of me.

READER: What you just said is a tremendous realization. It's important to liberate ourselves from the approval of others and understand it's just a projection of whether or not we trust ourselves. We each have to become responsible for ourselves and not blame it on others. There is no freedom without responsibility, and for each of us the rest of the world represents responsibility.

TOM: I want to get away from all that. Why should I be liable for someone else's shit?

READER: Because no one lives in a vacuum- you have chosen to let certain things happen and now that they've played out you don't like what you've gotten. Whose fault is that?

TOM: You're the one offering Spiritual Guidance, what should I do next?

READER: What do you want? Do you want to have a man-to-man relationship with your Father? Do you really want to be a musician? Do you want to have a mature and loving relationship with another human being? You tell me.

TOM: I want to be happy and do what's right.

READER: You want to be happy? Then do what "feels" right to you. Like I've asked you already, what do you want?

TOM: I guess it's more about what I don't want. You're making everything sound so clear and simple; do this or do that and something happens and then fix it, or whatever. But it's rarely that easy. You do shit and people get pissed, then someone does something back to you and it hurts. How does any of this crap ever get fixed?

READER: I don't know if anything can be fixed if you mean, "undone". But we do have the power to redeem ourselves, to make new choices, to make new starts, to let go of the past. That's the whole Christ metaphor, isn't it? We can be forgiven and we can forgive others, but whatever has happened can't be undone.

TOM: You can talk about forgiveness, but do we ever really forget?

READER: By remembering you keep something that happened in the past alive in the present. After that it's only a very short step to mistaking the present for the past. Then one is living an illusion.

TOM: How do we tell the difference between what we're remembering and what's happening if it seems like the same thing is happening over and over again?

READER: By doing something different. That's what Karma is, the endless cycles of cause and effect until we realize we've just been making the same choices over and over and expecting a different result.

TOM: Like the way my Father and I manage to always push each other's buttons even if we're trying to be nice to one another?

READER: Precisely.

TOM: So how do we change?

READER: By not wanting each other to be different...

TOM: I don't know what you mean.

READER: The root of the conflict between you and your Father is that both of you want the other one to change, but neither of you are willing to change yourselves. Try accepting your Father for who he is and then don't edit yourself. I don't mean wait to see what he does and then do the opposite to spite him. Let him be and then do what seems right independently of what he sets off in you. Maybe sometimes you guys could actually agree if you weren't always prepared to disagree?

TOM: I never thought of it that way before, but now that you mention it....

READER: Let me tell you a little story. A couple of years ago I was in Journal Square Station and sitting in a PATH train waiting for it to depart. When I looked to my right I saw a Young Black Woman and a Young White Man walk in and sit down together. After they started talking, I turned away and looked out the window across from me. A few moments later when I looked back in their direction I saw that same man and woman walk in and sit down again exactly as they did before.

TOM: Oh shit! Really?

READER: Yeah, I saw the same thing happen twice, but rather than wrack my brain to try and figure it out, I instead admitted to myself that I didn't know what the hell it meant. I know what I saw and left it at that.

For the rest of the day I felt weird, but it didn't feel bad. In fact, in a strange way I felt kind of exhilarated. The bottom line is that over the ensuing weeks I began to notice subtle changes in both my awareness and my emotional state. My work with clients started to get clearer and deeper so that eventually I came to look at that incident I just described as an upgrade of my operating system. It was at that point that I began to look at the whole issue of knowledge and enlightenment quite differently than I had before. Evolution is not a direct, logical, and cumulative progression, but rather a Quantum Leap at an opportune moment and then a process of reverse engineering to a new level of stasis. In other words, I just let the whole incident happen and then moved on, for to try and explain to myself what I wasn't ready to understand would've only amounted to denying the experience! I could only come to comprehend what I'd seen in terms of letting myself be changed by it over time. Now I can look back and see quite clearly how much different I am.

TOM: That would've freaked me out.

READER: It did freak me out, but anything less would not have challenged me in the same way. It's not important that you fully understand and accept right now whatever you've experienced here today, instead let it unsettle you and see what happens over time. You will come to understand what has gone on here and who that person was you saw inside of yourself during your visualization. Just try to be patient and see what you turn into over the ensuing weeks and months.

TOM: I don't know….. but hey, maybe you're right?

(At this point the phone alarm goes off with the theme from "The X Files" and The Reader reaches over to turn it off.)

READER: We're out of time. Do you have any last questions?

TOM: (With a mischievous look in his eye)
So you don't believe in The Illuminati or what Beelzebuddy has to say about them?

(The Reader smiles at Tom as though he were a small child)

READER: Over the years I've seen enough weird stuff to believe anything is possible. The word Illuminati means "The Enlightened Ones." My advice would be to concern yourself with your own clarity and evolution and then who knows, maybe someday you'll get to meet one of the Illuminati and then you can ask them yourself if they're real?

TOM: Would they admit if they were Illuminati? They take an oath of secrecy, don't they?
Wouldn't that mean …….

(At this point the song "Somebody to Love" by The Jefferson Airplane starts playing over the sound system, drowning out the rest of what Tom is saying as the two men stand up from the table and exit the stage.)

END

www.ingramcontent.com/pod-product-compliance
Lightning Source LLC
Chambersburg PA
CBHW060035050426
42448CB00012B/3014